Blaze the Trail of Equipoise

Blaze the Trail of Equipoise

A BOOK OF CONTEMPLATIONS

A SIDDHA YOGA PUBLICATION
PUBLISHED BY THE SYDA FOUNDATION

The cover photo captures the sun rising during monsoon season on a contemplation path around Dakshinkashi, the south field at Gurudev Siddha Peeth, Ganeshpuri, India. Gurudev Siddha Peeth is the mother ashram of Siddha Yoga and the site of Swami Muktananda's Samadhi Shrine.

ACKNOWLEDGMENTS
Grateful appreciation goes to Lissa Feldman for her careful research, to David Schneider for the cover photo, to Cheryl Crawford for the design, to Sushila Traverse for coordinating production, and to all those others who offered their service with love.

Jane Ferrar, Editor

Permissions appear on pg. 72

Printed in the United States of America

First edition 1995

ISBN 0-911307-40-0

CONTENTS

THE TRADITION of SIDDHA YOGA

Siddha Yoga is a path of spiritual unfoldment that is inspired by the grace and guidance of an enlightened Master, known as a Siddha Guru.

A Siddha Guru is one who has the power and knowledge to give others the inner experience of God. Through the transmission of grace, known as Shaktipat initiation, the Siddha Master awakens a seeker's inner spiritual energy. Having walked the spiritual path to its final goal, Siddha Gurus dedicate their life to helping others complete the same journey.

Swami Chidvilasananda, widely known as Gurumayi, is a Siddha Guru. Since early childhood, she has been a disciple of the Siddha Master Swami Muktananda Paramahamsa (1908-1982). It was he who invested Swami Chidvilasananda with the knowledge, power, and authority of the ancient tradition of Siddhas.

During his lifetime Swami Muktananda became adept at many of the classical paths of yoga, yet he said his spiritual journey did not truly begin until Bhagawan Nityananda, one of the great saints of modern India, awakened him to the experience of the supreme Power within himself.

Bhagawan Nityananda chose Swami Muktananda as his successor and directed him to bring Shaktipat initiation and the timeless practices of yoga to seekers everywhere. The path Swami Muktananda taught, which introduced the wisdom and disciplines of the ancient sages to the modern world, came to be known as Siddha Yoga. Gurumayi continues in her Guru's tradition, offering the teachings of the Siddhas and Shaktipat initiation to seekers around the world.

Through Siddha Yoga and its principal practices of meditation, chanting, contemplation, and selfless service, thousands of people from many different traditions and cultures have discovered within themselves the source of lasting happiness and peace: the awareness that we are not separate from God.

FOREWORD

From the most ancient of times, teachers in the various religious traditions of the world have instructed spiritual seekers to practice a special kind of contemplation in which aspirants read or listen attentively to concise passages of scripture or to powerful words of sages. Seekers then quietly and with deep reverence reflect on the inner significance of the teachings and search within themselves for ways to apply those lessons in their own lives.

In Christian monasticism, for example, monks and nuns who yearn for a taste of God's presence practice what is known as *lectio divina*, holy reading, in which they prayerfully meditate on short passages from scripture as a way to gain inspiration and deeper wisdom. Tradition regards the imbibing of sacred truths in this way as nourishment of the soul and in fact quite vividly describes the process as *ruminatio,* literally a slow and repeated chewing of the sacred words that leads to the release of their full flavor.

In India, such a rumination on a sacred text or lesson from one's spiritual teacher may be said to lead to the tasting of *rasa,* the ambrosial essence of the sublime. According to Abhinavagupta, the great Kashmiri Siddha of the eleventh century, *rasāsvāda* is similar to *brahmāsvāda:* the taste of such an essence is comparable to the taste of the Divine itself.

But virtually all religious traditions in India hold that such a nectarean flavor cannot be tasted without diligent and attentive spiritual discipline. Such discipline necessarily includes a number of different yet related practices, one of the most honored of which has always been that of *svādhyāya,* a term we may translate as "self-reflection" or "recitation by oneself." Undertaking *svādhyāya,* a spiritual seeker quietly chants mantras, recites *sūtras,* sings sacred *gītās,* studies texts, or repeats words spoken by the Guru. While doing so, he or she inwardly contemplates their deeper meaning.

The *Bhagavad Gītā* reports Krishna's teaching to Arjuna that *svādhyāya* is one of the divine virtues. In the second century B.C., the great sage Patanjali saw *svādhyāya* to be so important that he listed it among five primary yogic disciplines without which there can be no true spiritual growth (the other four are moral and physical purity, the cultivation of inner contentment or equanimity, fervent dedication to one's practice, and devotion to God). Patanjali taught that *svādhyāya* joins with fervent practice and devotion to God to form what he called the "yoga of action" and that the study of sacred words is such an effective practice that it leads to communion with the Divine. In roughly the eighth century, the teacher

Vedavyasa similarly asserted that "the gods, the visionary seers, and the Siddhas themselves become visible to one who practices *svādhyāya*."

But the spiritual traditions of India also hold that, having heard or read a powerful teaching, a seeker must endeavor to bring the liberating insights and transformative truths presented by those words into effect in his or her life. Otherwise the words merely entertain, mystify, or even clutter the mind. The Siddhas teach us that true contemplation is part of a process: hearing, contemplating, understanding, imbibing, becoming. As Swami Muktananda has said, "Knowledge that is not put into action is a burden."

The contemplations in this book are tools to help you in your own version of *svādhyāya*. You may wish to focus on one particular passage for a period of time. Memorize it, perhaps, or write it down so that you can carry it with you wherever you go. Record your thoughts inspired by the wisdom reflected in these teachings; you will surely delight in the bright gems you thus have mined from the quiet integrity of your own soul.

This collection is part of a series, each book of which contains a set of contemplations centered on a different aspect of the spiritual life. These contemplations are not merely pleasant or interesting thoughts; they are selections from scriptures as well as lessons from philosophers and teachings from ancient and modern saints. They possess *śabda-vīrya*, the "potency of sacred words," the power of which can transform your life and strengthen your spiritual discipline.

Contemplating them, we somehow inwardly recognize the Truth these words outwardly express. This is because the same Truth lies within each of us. It may be that much of the time that Truth is, for us, still vague and unformed because we have not found the words with which to express it. These contemplations give us those words. Reflecting on them can therefore inspire the awakening and blossoming of our own inner wisdom.

Ruminate slowly on these teachings. Relish their delectable essence. Let them nourish you.

William K. Mahony
Department of Religion
Davidson College
Davidson, North Carolina

INTRODUCTION

The theme of the contemplations in this book was introduced by Swami Chidvilasananda in her New Year's message for 1995: "Blaze the trail of equipoise and enter the heart, the divine splendor."

Gurumayi has spoken on this theme many times, in both formal and informal settings. On one occasion, she said, "The message for this year requests you to cultivate the state of equipoise, so that you may drink the elixir of the splendor of the heart. Of course, this experience of inner stability is not only necessary this year, it is something that must be in your possession at all times: past, present, and future." Another time Gurumayi noted the important place of contemplation itself in the cultivation of that inner stillness. "If you truly want to blaze the trail of equipoise," she said, "then resolve the conflicting thoughts in your mind with the wisdom of contemplation."

The passages in the following pages can help you as you work toward the state of inner stillness. As you read them, keep in mind that these words come from a state of deep love and Truth.

Many of us want fervently to taste God's presence but find that the outside world and our own personal concerns press onto us, keeping us from reaching the inner stillness necessary to do so. The wise ones teach us, though, that true discipline is that which we undertake while continuing to perform all of our responsibilities. Stillness does indeed help us in our discipline. But it also takes discipline to be still. There cannot be one without the other. In some ways they are the same thing. In the *Bhagavad Gītā*, Krishna teaches Arjuna: *samatva yoga ucyate*, equanimity is discipline itself.

Gurumayi uses the word equipoise.

What an exquisite choice of a word! The first part, *equi*poise, connotes a balance of one's being. The second part, equi*poise,* suggests dignity, strength, and the integrity not only of one's inner being but also of one's relationships to others. Equipoise thus describes an internal balance that comes not from a static lack of movement and change but rather from the courage, confidence, and inner calmness to live in harmony with the complexities of life. Having cultivated equipoise, one is not pulled apart by the pressures of life and is therefore able to offer one's genuinely loving attentiveness to the importance of life's details. Perhaps this is what Galileo had in mind when he said: "The sun, with all those planets revolving around it and dependent on it, can still ripen a bunch of grapes as if it had nothing else in the universe to do."

The five sections of this book remind us of five aspects of equipoise and give us the tools to make this divine quality our own. The first section points out just what it is we are to work toward: inner balance, harmony, evenness of mind and spirit, stillness, discrimination. Lessons in the second section teach us that in order to gain this equipoise we must quiet our restless and impatient minds.

Contemplating the passages in the third section, we remember that in order to calm the spirit we must renounce self-centered activity and free ourselves of all forms of craving. The fourth part reminds us that when we undertake such discipline, we experience deep contentment and can truly celebrate our lives and those of others. The contemplations in the fifth section return us to the understanding that all of this takes place in the context of loving devotion to God. It also recalls to us just where the foundation of such equipoise stands: it is in the heart, the divine splendor.

The powerful words of these contemplations thus teach us that equipoise both emerges from and brings us back to the holiness of the heart itself. May we truly immerse ourselves in these teachings and taste the graceful love that resides in that splendid realm.

WKM

1.

EQUIPOISE

Dear Seekers!

Equipoise is what we should possess, disharmony what we should renounce.

One Reality is the true nature of all. It is, indeed, the Absolute.

This is the message of all the saints.

Swami Muktananda

In this world of diversity,
only equipoise
can bring about sanity;
only equipoise
can open the door
to God's world.

What is equipoise?

A balanced state of mind,
evenness of temper,
inner composure,
unwavering steadiness;
a state in which
everything is tranquil
although it is in motion;
in which everything moves,
yet remains serene.

Swami Chidvilasananda

*Continual change
is a law of nature.*

*If you just go along with it
like driftwood on the tides of the sea
you cannot bring to light
the Truth that is hidden
in your own being.*

*It is not that you must oppose
the law of nature,
but that you must become still
within yourself.*

You may be looking everywhere
but there is stillness in your seeing.
You may be hearing everything,
but there is stillness in your hearing.
You may be walking or working—
even then there is inner stillness.

If you want to experience the Truth
there has to be
complete stillness within.

The deeper your stillness,
the stronger your foundation.

Swami Chidvilasananda

A perfect sphere,
eternally resting
in precise equipoise,
constantly exults
while circling
in its solitude.[1]

Empedocles

$\mathcal{S}$omeone once said to Rumi,
"If you believe in silence,
why have you done nothing
but talk and talk
and write and sing and dance?"

He laughed and said,
"The radiant one inside me
has never said a word."

*O*n the one hand,
it is amazing
that such a state — equipoise — exists,
a state in which
all the diversified worlds
come to rest.

On the other hand,
without one's willingness
to do whatever is necessary
to attain such a state,
without constantly invoking grace,
it is almost as if
that state were not real.

So the state of equipoise
is both existent and nonexistent.
It depends on your point of view.

It is yours
if you are ready to seek it.
If you deny it
or hold back from it,
it might as well not exist.

Swami Chidvilasananda

O Lord,
calm the waves of this heart;
calm its tempests.

Calm thyself, O my soul,
so that the divine can act in thee,
so that God may repose in thee,
so that His peace may cover thee.

O Lord,
make us understand
that the world cannot give us peace,
that you alone grant peace.
Let us know the truth
of thy promise:
that the whole world
cannot steal thy peace.

Kierkegaard

2.
A MIND WITH PATIENCE

The state of equipoise
is inherent in all beings.
Why, then, does a person
continually live in misery?

How is it possible?

It is because of the mind,
the confused and deluded mind.

A fickle mind
will never let you see
your own divinity.

A mind like this
must be invited to become immersed
in the sādhana of equipoise.

Swami Chidvilasananda

A turbulent mind,
a spinning, restless mind, is weak.
A strong mind is a still mind;
such a mind can accomplish anything.

Beings who pursued sādhana
and made their minds quiet
became so supremely happy
that their joy remained
even if they possessed nothing.

You can experience this for yourself.

Just for a few moments
make your mind still:
you will experience a joy
that can be experienced
in no other way.

Swami Muktananda

*It is very hard for people
to understand what it means
to have a silent mind.
They immediately conclude
that such a mind
has "No thoughts,
no thoughts at all."*

*Truly speaking, a quiet mind
is a mind with patience.*

You do not need
to root out all thoughts.
Some thoughts are quite sacred:
they take you to God.

So, having a silent mind
does not mean erasing
the light of the mind.
A silent mind, a still mind,
has patience.

Swami Chidvilasananda

The mind that is established in virtue
and carries the bundle of patience
cannot be shaken by mishaps
but remains unmoved
like a plant in a painting.

Yoga Vāsiṣṭha

*S*omeone once asked
Swami Muktananda:

"Tell me, does your mind think?"

Baba smiled and said,
"Only when I ask it to."

*There is something beyond the mind
that abides in silence within the mind:
it is the supreme mystery
beyond thought.*

*Let one's mind and subtle body
rest upon that and on nothing else.*

Maitri Upaniṣad

When the mind is still but not lazy,
when it reaches the thought free state,
you will be able to glimpse
the brilliance of the soul.

The Self is there, God is there.

It is not necessary
to carry out a search for Him:
God is already there.

Swami Muktananda

According to the knowers of the Truth
it is God who lives within the mind.
Just think: God living in your mind!
The mind cannot grasp Him,
and yet it is only able to think
because of His power.

This is very humbling
for those who believe
that they are the thinkers,
that they are the knowers,
that they are the doers.

But for those who aspire to know life
beyond the fluctuations of the mind
it is a very beautiful statement
and a very powerful experience.

Swami Chidvilasananda

O mind,
who has not come under your thumb?
You make everyone in this world dance
until they become exhausted.
Only saints can make you dance:
they grasp you by the ankles
and hold you fast.

O mind,
when you stop flying about
then one experiences tranquility.
A person who seizes control of you
becomes free from agitation
and experiences only supreme bliss.
The one who holds you in his pocket
is indeed fortunate.

Bhartrihari

With great subtlety
try to understand the mind.

The mind is Consciousness
in a limited form.

When Consciousness
becomes contracted,
it becomes the mind.
The moment
it gives up its contraction
it evolves,
it expands,
it becomes free,
and then it is
supreme Consciousness again.

You are not your thoughts.
You are the Witness,
the Knower of your thoughts.
You are the perceiver
of your thoughts.
You understand them.

The Knower is Consciousness.
Understand that you are that Knower.

Swami Muktananda

A person cannot see his own image
in flowing water
but sees it in water that is tranquil.

Only that which remains at rest itself
can become the resting place
for all those who wish to seek rest.

Confucius

3.

THE POWER
OF RENUNCIATION

If you keep trying to satisfy desires,
they will blaze up higher and higher
until they swallow you completely.

The only way to become peaceful
is to become free of desires,
and the only way to be free of them
is to recognize and control them.

When desires come up in the mind,
you must be able to let them go.
This is what discipline means.

Swami Muktananda

*A*bandonment of desires
is called śama, control of the mind.

Restraint of the external functions
of the organs is called dama.

Turning away completely
from all sense objects
is the height of uparati, equipoise.[2]

And patient endurance
of all sorrow or pain
is known as titīkṣa, forbearance,
which is conducive to happiness.

Shankaracharya

Excessive pains and pleasures
are rightly to be regarded
as the greatest diseases
to which the soul is liable.
For a man who is in great joy
or in great pain,
in his unseasonable eagerness
to attain the one
and to avoid the other,
is not able to see or to hear
anything rightly;
but he is mad,
and is at the time
utterly incapable
of any participation in reason.

Plato

*Even as rain breaks through
an ill-thatched house,
passions will break through
an ill-guarded mind.*

Dhammapada

Only the power of renunciation
can soothe your troubled mind.

How does this become a reality?

*First you weigh the importance
of your state of mind
against the temporary relief
of expressing emotions
such as anger.*

*You ask yourself,
"What matters most?
Equipoise or retaliation?
Staying even or getting even?"*

For better or worse
you have to make your choice.
Only then will you be able
to deal with any situation
calmly and effectively.

Developing the potential
for choosing correctly
is the same as developing
the attitude of renunciation.

Swami Chidvilasananda

When a person
has no self control
he has no ability to endure hardship.
He weeps when he has to face sickness
or other worldly difficulties.

A person
who has developed self control
can endure anything joyfully.
He has the strength to bear
the worst difficulties with equanimity.

For this reason, discipline is a great
attainment and a great friend.

Swami Muktananda

Discipline
is not holding your body tense
or depriving yourself
of the pleasures of this world.
It's a way of thinking.
It's becoming aware of
what is śreyas—beneficial,
and what is preyas—pleasant.[3]

When you understand
what is truly beneficial
over a long period of time,
you are able to take responsibility
for your own life.

Swami Chidvilasananda

A renunciant visiting the palace of a king prostrated himself at the monarch's feet calling out, "Salutations to you, O great renunciant!"

The king, surprised by the greeting, replied, "But you are the holy man, the man of renunciation. For God you have renounced this entire world! I live in great comfort; all my desires are fulfilled. Why do you call me 'renunciant'? You are the renunciant, not I."

"Ah, king," responded the ascetic, "You are the greater renunciant. For the sake of the world you have given up God—who is everything."

Traditional Tale

The power of renunciation
allows you to experience
true freedom.

The attitude of renunciation,
of letting go,
keeps you from being enmeshed
in other people's opinions,
ideas and circumstances,
and in the ups and downs
of your own moods
and of others' emotions.

The state of equipoise
empowers renunciation.
And renunciation
continually leads you
to the realm of equipoise.

Swami Chidvilasananda

For one who craves nothing,
who has subdued his senses and mind,
who is even-minded toward all
and is satisfied with Me,
all four directions are full of bliss.

Uddhava Gītā

4.
THE STILLNESS
OF CONTENTMENT

Be content with what you have;
rejoice in the way things are.
When you realize
there is nothing lacking,
the whole world belongs to you.

Lao Tsu

*From contentment
unsurpassed happiness
is gained.*

Patanjali's
Yoga Sūtras

*Contentment is like a serene lake
that reflects the sun, the moon,
the stars, the trees, the birds—
everything that comes near it.*

*It is totally full within itself
and also reflects the beauty of nature.*

*As calm as it is,
it allows the water creatures
to move about
without being disturbed by them.
The fish move, the weeds move,
yet the lake is very calm.*

*It also offers its own nature,
contentment, to those who are disturbed
or anguished or simply lonely
and who find solace in the company
of its still waters.*

A seeker, too,
must cultivate
the stillness of contentment.

Contentment is the garment
of one who has become
completely established
in the heart of all hearts.

Swami Chidvilasananda

The man of contemplation
walks alone.
He lives desireless
amidst the objects of desire.
The Self alone
is his eternal satisfaction.
He himself exists
as the Self in all.

He has no riches
yet is always contented.
He is helpless
yet of mighty power.
He enjoys nothing
yet is continually rejoicing.
He has no equal
yet sees all men as his equals.

Shankaracharya

The state of equality consciousness,
seeing the One in everything,
gives rise to unearthly joy.

To grow in that experience,
perform your sādhana diligently:
listen to the wisdom of the great beings,
meditate on the great truths,
continually contemplate
the deeper meanings of the teachings
and translate them into daily actions.

This is the path to even-mindedness.

Swami Chidvilasananda

Our endless sufferings
are the roots of illness.

When mortals are alive,
they worry about death.
When they're full,
they worry about hunger.
Theirs is the Great Uncertainty.

But sages don't consider the past.
And they don't worry about the future.
Nor do they cling to the present.
From moment to moment
they follow the Way.

If you haven't awakened
to this great Truth,
you'd better look for a teacher
on earth or in the heavens.

Bodhidharma

*You are completely freed from anxieties
when you see one who is undaunted
by the waves of the world;*

*one who is detached
from all pettiness
and who remains centered
in the knowledge of God
no matter what the situation;*

*one who has acquired
the glow of Truthfulness;
who has become anchored
in selfless service;
whose only purpose
is to spread God's love
and whose energy
is as clear as spring water.*

The presence of such a being
has an immediate effect.
You experience yourself
as enfolded
in a blanket of perfect calm.

You feel so blessed
to have laid your eyes
on someone who lives
with so much grace and wisdom.

It increases your longing
to blaze the trail to equipoise
and to make this state your own.

Swami Chidvilasananda

I love Master Ming.
He is free like the wind,
known by all below heaven.

When young, with rosy cheeks
he threw away comfort and rank;
now, with white hair
he lies peacefully
under pines and cloud.

Intoxicated under the moonlight
his presence strikes all who come near.
Carefree among the flowers
he depends on no one.

How can I scale
such a high mountain peak?
By staying here, below,
bowing to his sweet perfume.

Li Po

I saw all kinds of things;
I accepted some and rejected others.
When Guru Nityananda showed me
the underlying Truth,
I saw that the accepted
and the rejected were one.

Muktananda rested in Nityananda
and all the fatigue
of his spiritual journey
melted away.

Swami Muktananda

Once a Muslim priest
asked Rabi'a of Basri
"Does God speak to you?"

Rabi'a answered,
"Does one have to talk to God?
I keep looking at Him,
and He keeps looking at me.
What could be more sublime?

Seeing Him,
I become utterly content,
and then He is happy with me.
What could be more wonderful
than perfect contentment?"

5.
ENTER THE HEART,
THE DIVINE SPLENDOR

*There are scriptures
that can cleanse a person
of the three impurities.*[4]
*And there are those yogins and paṇḍits
who have mastered these scriptures.
But the only ones truly equipoised
are those devoted to You.*

Utpaladeva

The power of devotion
is very purifying.
If you let devotion lead the way
you always find yourself
in a state of equipoise.

Your mind becomes
more and more mature.

You honor everyone you encounter.
You treat every object with respect.
Nothing is insignificant for you.
Every word takes on a rich meaning.

Wherever you look,
you try to see the presence of God.

This is true devotion.

Swami Chidvilasananda

Always remember God.
Remember Him from within,
not just on the outside.

Only when a person thinks of God
as being somewhere out there,
separate from him,
does he get irritated with other people.
Only then does he become agitated.

If a person were to experience
God within himself,
then he would naturally
experience the same love
in everyone else, too.

Swami Muktananda

The love of God,
unutterable and perfect,
flows into a pure soul
the way that light
rushes into a transparent object.

The more love that it finds,
the more it gives itself;
so that, as we grow clear and open,
the more complete the joy of heaven is.

And the more souls
who resonate together,
the greater the intensity of their love,
and, mirror-like, each soul
reflects the other.

Dante

O Lord, You are in every country,
in every costume.
Your names are countless,
but You are only one.
The whole universe is Your stage,
and in the play of this entire drama
there is only You.

O Lord, You alone exist.
My Guru has given me
this divine vision
through His grace.

O dear ones, chant His name;
repeat His name
and become one with Him.
Experience the Lord in your heart.

Tukadyadas

I understood
that love comprised all vocations,
that love was everything,
that it embraced all times and places....
In a word,
that it was eternal!

Then,
in the excess of my delirious joy,
I cried out:
O Jesus, my Love...
my vocation,
at last I have found it...
my vocation is love!

Thérèse of Lisieux

For one intent on being entirely
in the highest perfection,
the nature of which
is the state of being liberated
while still alive,
there is nothing at all
that is of any use;
except for the attainment
of the seed of the Heart.

Abhinavagupta

The little space within the heart
is as great as this vast universe.
The heavens and the earth are there,
and the sun, and the moon, and the stars;
fire and lightning and winds are there;
and all that now is and all that is not:
for the whole universe is in Him
and He dwells within our heart.

Chāndogya Upaniṣad

His Light rose,
I found it in my own heart –
It is now my Light
you see shining!

Araqi

The shadows of evening grow deep
while love comes in
to soothe every mind and body.

Look out toward the West
and see the fading light of the sun.
Look within yourself
and see an endless sky of light.
Drink the nectar
from the petals of your heart
and let the waves
sweep through your body.

What glory in that ocean! Listen!
The sound of conches!
The sound of bells! Kabir says,
"O brother, listen! The Lord of all
is playing His song within you!"

Kabir

The sādhana *of equipoise*
will uplift you every step of the way.
Certainly,
it will unveil the face
of the Truth for you.

Then you will inhale
the most extraordinary fragrance
emanating from everything
you perceive.

And your entire being
will shimmer in the light.

I encourage you all
to blaze the trail of equipoise
and enter the heart,
the divine splendor.

Swami Chidvilasananda

Notes

1 (Page 6) Empedocles, an early Greek philosopher, drew his observations from nature and described the point of stillness at the center of the universe as a sphere "quietly rejoicing in its own solitude."

2 (Page 27) While practicing *śama* and *dama*, the seeker makes an effort to restrain the outgoing tendencies of the mind. In *uparati*, the equipoise of the mind becomes natural and spontaneous and no further striving is needed to gain it.

3 (Page 33) *Śreyas* is that which proves to be beneficial over time. *Preyas* is that which seems to be pleasant in the moment but ultimately proves harmful.

4 (Page 52) The three impurities are *āṇava mala*, a sense of separation from God; *mayīya mala,* a sense of difference between oneself and others; and *karma mala*, the sense that "I am the doer."

Glossary

sādhana: A spiritual discipline or path; practices, both physical and mental, on the spiritual path.

samādhi shrine: A sanctuary built at the burial place of a saint or great *yogin* after he has taken *māhāsamādhi* (lit. the great *samādhi*) or final union of the individual consciousness with the Absolute.

sūtra: A scriptural aphorism; the seed form of a philosophic point that can be unfolded infinitely through contemplation.

gītā: (lit. song) A scripture in verse that can be recited by chanting.

paṇḍit: A Hindu religious scholar; a priest.

yogin: A practicioner of yoga, who through discipline attains higher states of consciousness.

Authors and Scriptures

Abhinavagupta (eleventh century), a sage of
the Shaiva philosophy.

Araqi, Fakhruddin (1213-1289), a Sufi Master
who spontaneously composed poems as he
sang for his disciples.

Bhartrihari, a king of ancient India who
renounced his throne to become a great yogi.

Bodhidharma (440-528), the patriarch of Zen
Buddhism and of the martial art Kung-Fu.

Chāndogya Upaniṣad, a part of the *Sama Veda*
and one of the most lyrical of the Upanishadic
texts.

Confucius (551-479 B.C.), founder of the
Chinese philosophy that bears his name and
that emphasizes kindness, love, and proper
moral conduct.

Dante Alighieri (1265-1321), an Italian poet
who described the depths and heights
of human experience in his masterpiece
The Divine Comedy.

Dhammapada ("The Path of Virtue"), a collection of verses outlining the Buddhist system of ethics.

Empedocles (490-430 B.C.), a Greek philosopher and poet who wrote *Peri Physeos* ("On Nature"), putting forward the then novel theory that matter is not created or destroyed but only transformed.

Jnaneshwar Maharaj (1275-1296), a great saint of India whose *Jñāneśwarī* is a magnificent commentary in Marathi verse on the *Bhagavad Gītā*.

Kabir (1440-1518), a poet and saint who worked as a simple weaver in the North Indian city of Benaras.

Kierkegaard, Soren (1813-1855), a mystical Danish philosopher, regarded as the founder of Existentialism.

Lao Tsu (sixth century B.C.), Chinese philosopher and purported author of the classic scripture of Taoism, *Tao Te Ching* ("The Way and Its Power").

Li Po (701-762), a mystical poet of the Chinese T'ang Dynasty.

Maitri Upaniṣad, a text found at the end of the *Kriṣṇa Yajur Veda.*

Patanjali (second century B.C.), great sage of India and author of the *Yoga Sūtras.*

Plato (429-347 B.C.), a Greek philosopher whose writings have influenced Western philosophy for twenty five hundred years.

Rabi'a of Basri (714-801), a great Sufi poet and mystic, sold into slavery as a child. Her sanctity so impressed the man who bought her that he set her free.

Rumi, Jalaluddin (1207-1273), the most eminent saint of Persia and Turkey, transformed from a sober scholar into an intoxicated lover of God after one meeting with his Master, Shams-i-Tabriz.

Shankaracharya (780-820), a sage who spread the philosophy of Advaita Vedanta, absolute non-dualism, throughout India.

Thérèse of Lisieux (1873-1897), a French nun who led a brief and passionately mystical life.

Tukadyadas or Tukadoji Maharaj (twentieth century), a saint from Maharashtra, India. He used to chant *bhajans,* devotional songs, with Swami Muktananda.

Uddhava Gītā, the final teachings of Lord Krishna to his friend and disciple Uddhava, found at the end of the *Śrīmad Bhāgavatam.*

Utpaladeva (tenth century), one of the great Shaiva philosophers of Kashmir.

Yoga Vāsiṣṭha, an ancient text recording dialogues between the Indian sage Vasishtha and his disciple, Lord Rama.

Guide to Sanskrit Pronunciation

Vowels

Sanskrit vowels are categorized as either long or short. In English transliteration, the long vowels are marked with a bar above the letter and are pronounced twice as long as a short vowel. The vowels *e* and *o* are also pronounced like long vowels.

Short:	Long:
a as in c*u*p	*ā* as in c*a*lm
i as in g*i*ve	*ī* as in s*ee*n
u as in f*u*ll	*ū* as in sch*oo*l

Consonants

The main difference between Sanskrit and English pronunciation of consonants is in the aspirated letters. In Sanskrit these are pronounced with a definite *h* sound. The following list covers variations of pronunciation for most aspirated consonants found in this book:

ṭh as in an*th*ill	*ṇ* as in o*n*e
dh as in a*dh*ere	*ś* as in *s*ure
bh as in clu*bh*ouse	*ṣ* as in *sh*ine

For a detailed pronunciation guide, see *The Nectar of Chanting,* published by SYDA Foundation

Copyright Acknowledgments

Further Reading

SWAMI MUKTANANDA

Play of Consciousness
From the Finite to the Infinite
Where Are You Going?
I Have Become Alive
The Perfect Relationship
Reflections of the Self
Secret of the Siddhas
I Am That
Kundalini
Mystery of the Mind
Does Death Really Exist?
Light on the Path
In the Company of a Siddha
Lalleshwari
Mukteshwari
Meditate

SWAMI CHIDVILASANANDA

My Lord Loves a Pure Heart
Kindle My Heart
Ashes at My Guru's Feet

You may learn more about the teachings and
practices of Siddha Yoga Meditation by contacting:

SYDA Foundation
371 Brickman Rd.
South Fallsburg, NY 12779-0600, USA

Tel: (914) 434-2000
or

Gurudev Siddha Peeth
P.O. Ganeshpuri
PIN 401 206
District Thana
Maharashtra, India

For further information about books in print by
Swami Muktananda and Swami Chidvilasananda,
and editions in translation, please contact:

Siddha Yoga Meditation Bookstore
371 Brickman Rd.
South Fallsburg, NY 12779-0600, USA

Tel: (914) 434-0124